Simple Salon Marketing

The 2-Step System to Get New Clients and Make More Money

By
Dustin NcCorchuk

Copyright © 2022. Dustin NcCorchuk.

All rights reserved. No part of this book may be reproduced, stored in a retrieval system or transmitted, in any form or by any means—other than for "fair use" as brief quotations, embodied in reviews and articles—without the prior written consent of the publisher.

Disclaimer: The author makes no guarantees to the results you'll achieve by reading this book. All business requires risk and hard work. Results may vary when starting a new business or marketing strategy.

Salon Growth Academy

SalonGrowthAcademy.com

To my wife, Rachel. You are an inspiration for hairstylists everywhere. No one does hair and cares for clients like you.

Table of Contents

Introduction 8
1 The Marketing Dilemma and How We Overcame It 13
2 The 3 Strategies to Grow Your Hair Business 19
3 The Buyer's Journey Marketing Funnel 24
4 The Website Philosophy 30
5 Choosing Website Images 35
6 Getting Started With Squarespace 40
7 The Basics of Editing in Squarespace 45
8 The Hero Section 49
9 The FOMO & Value Proposition Sections 53
10 The Authority Section 60
11 The Action Steps Section 65
12 The Testimonial Section 68
13 The Cover Letter Section 72
14 The Lead Generation Section 74
15 My Case For Online Scheduling 76
16 Getting Website Visitors 83
17 Hire Dustin For Your Salon Marketing 92

Introduction: For the Hairstylist Struggling to Fill Your Chair

How to read this book: This book exists for 2 reasons. Reason 1: To empower you to design a beautiful website for your business and drive potential clients to your website so you can grow your business. Reason #2: So you will hire me and my team to implement everything you learn here if you feel you can't do it on your own.

My honest desire is to help you as a hairstylist or salon/spa owner to get more clients quickly. And if you read this book in its entirety, you will have a straightforward blueprint to do just that without spending a ton of time on your marketing and without having to become a tech wizard.

First, I will get you to take an honest look at where your business is currently. Maybe you are just starting your career, or perhaps you have been at it for a while but haven't cracked the code on consistently getting new clients to schedule an appointment with you.

I will make a case for creating a simple yet beautiful website as your primary marketing tool. I will also show you why your website is the answer to getting a full book of clients on autopilot. I will show you the elements of an effective website that turns visitors into clients so that you never have a problem attracting new clients again. And the best part? You can have your beautiful website up and running in the next 48 hours, saving you a ton of money and hassle! Visit SalonGrowthAcademy.com/website to preview the website I will help you build in this book.

In the last part of the book, I will give you a strategy for getting women in your area to visit your website so that you are getting new prospective clients to schedule an appointment with you every day. This is the method I personally used to start my hair salon from scratch and become fully booked in 6 months. I have done it repeatedly for each of our hairstylists and am confident that if I can do it in my small town, you can do it too, wherever you live.

This might sound like a lot, but the entirety of this book can be summed up into 3 key points:

1. Since the beginning of the internet, websites have been the #1 way for any local business to

build trust and authority, not your Instagram, Facebook, or Tik-Tok profiles.
2. The more people in your area who visit your website, the more appointments you will book and the more money you will make. In other words, more website visitors equals a full chair.
3. Automate that process, so your website does all the hustle for you…no more relying on business cards, Instagram, or promoting your referral program to grow your business.

This book is meant to be read like a manual giving actionable steps to implement in real-time. Thus, you should not read it while in bed. Instead, read it near your computer. And when you get to Part 3, where I talk about the 7 sections you need on your homepage, I challenge you to not move on to the next chapter until you have finished designing that section on your website. That way, when you finish reading this book, you will also have a finished website that you are proud of!

Above all, it is my sincere hope that you will use the blueprint I will show you and have a long successful career. If you are an independent hairstylist, you could use this blueprint to grow a multiple chair salon if you choose.

Yes, this is a salon marketing book. But really, it is a book about the path of least resistance to building a profitable hair business. A business of serving clients that brings you joy and financial security.

I consider it a privilege to share what I have learned with you over the last 10 years.

If you haven't already signed up for my Salon Website Academy online course, you will want to do that right away. This book will TELL you everything you need to know, and the course actually SHOWS you the step-by-step process of how to do it so you can look over my shoulder as I build a website from scratch. You can use my text and images for your website or take what you have learned and make it your own. Visit SalonGrowthAcademy.com to sign up.

Helping salon professionals like you build your website, drive new visitors to the website, and grow a thriving hair business is what I do best. I'm here to help. You can check out a complete list of my marketing services in the last chapter of this book or by going to SalonGrowthAcademy.com/contact

To your success!

Dustin NcCorchuk

Part 1: Marketing Strategies to Attract New Clients

1
The Marketing Dilemma and How We Overcame It

I think we need to begin with the problem. You spent a small fortune to go to beauty school (maybe still paying off loans) and continuing education courses. They taught you to cut and color hair and gave you a certificate, but they didn't teach you the most important part: How to get clients!

Trying to grow a full clientele on your own feels like being thrown into the deep end of the pool without knowing how to swim. You have probably tried growing your Instagram following, passing out business cards, and implementing a referral program. But nothing is growing your clientele fast enough.

And when you are renting a chair or working off of commission, you don't have time (or extra money) to make mistakes. You have bills to pay, a family to support, and goals to achieve. Nothing is more frustrating than 'going to work' and not making any money.

Well, that's the whole point of this book! I am tired of seeing 80% of hairstylists fail in the first 1-2 years because they couldn't fill their chair fast enough to make it in this industry.

In this chapter, I will break down the 3 simple strategies we use in our salon to consistently get new clients in our chair every day on demand. The best part about these strategies is they are simple, inexpensive, and automated.

More on that in a minute...but no, this is not getting cheap clients through Groupon or giving out discounts. It is not through passing out business cards, flyers, referral programs, or hustling at social gatherings. It is not through complicated technology or time-consuming social media posting. And most importantly, it is not through hiring an expensive marketing agency.

Some of these methods will get you a few clients here and there. But ultimately, they are a waste of your time, money, or just flat out aren't the answer to getting clients in your chair day in and day out.

Almost no hairstylists know how to do this stuff, but it's like a superpower once you learn it. Your schedule will be booked solid weeks in advance.

And after you have grown a full book of clients, if you'd like to open your own salon as we did, you can continue applying these secrets to book your employees solid as well.

If you commit to reading this short book and implementing what I teach you, I promise that you will have a full book of clients within the next 6 months. Fair enough?

Our Story

My amazing wife, Rachel (also a hairstylist), and I have owned and operated a hair salon for the last decade and are running a multiple 6-figure hair business per year. But I want to take you back to the beginning because it wasn't always rainbows and unicorns!

About 17 years ago, Rachel and I got married in the Seattle area and immediately moved across the country to Washington DC, where she attended beauty school. We literally packed up everything we owned (which wasn't much) in my parent's minivan and drove across the country. We were young, in love, and didn't have a care in the world!

We found a one-bedroom apartment. Rachel went to beauty school, and I got a job as a garbage truck driver. No, this wasn't my dream job, but remember, we were young and in love, and it was a good (temporary) job to pay the bills while Rachel went through beauty school.

Well, one thing led to another, and we found ourselves pregnant with our first son. What the heck happened to 'no kids for 5 years?' That was the plan...so how'd this happen (I know how it happened)? Still young...and in love, but things just got real!

Rachel hurried and finished up her beauty school hours, graduated, and we decided to move back to the west coast, where we could be closer to our family with our new little bundle of joy.

4 years later, still young...still in love…now with a 4-year-old and a 3-year-old. Rachel watches the kids and occasionally does hair for friends and family, and I am STILL driving garbage trucks. Not really what we had envisioned for our lives.

There was this discontentment lingering in both of us. I remember it like it was yesterday. It was a Sunday afternoon, and I asked Rachel, "How much longer are we going to do this?" Neither of us was doing what we wanted in life. We were just existing, and I came to the realization that if we didn't force a change, we would wake up 5 years down the road doing the same thing.

So we chose to take a risk. We decided to quit our jobs, move to a small town, and start a hair salon. That sounds like a solid plan, right? Our family thought we were crazy, but that's what we did. We moved our little family to a small town in Oregon, found a tiny 120 sq ft room inside an athletic club, installed a shampoo bowl and chair, and we were open for business.

I may have been young and naive, but I wasn't stupid. I did understand simple math. I knew that if Rachel has no clients in her chair, she makes no money which means no food, no rent..and that's no bueno. But if we could figure out a way to get even 2 cut and color clients in her chair each day, we could make it. I also understood that 80% of hairstylists fail in the first 18 months, and to not become one of those statistics, I needed to figure out the most effective way to get clients in her chair.

So, long story short, we tried everything you think you should do if you are starting a business. We made business cards and bought an ad in the local coupon book. We made a commercial for local TV, sent out postcards, and even gave out free haircuts to people we thought were influencers in the community.

We were willing to try *anything*, and unfortunately, with these methods, we only got a few new clients. More money was going out than coming in. We didn't have a lot of time left, and if we didn't turn this around, I was worried we would be one of the failed hairstylist statistics.

So I decided to try something new, and the results were amazing! Within 3 months, we supported ourselves entirely on Rachel's hair income. Within 6 months, Rachel's schedule was fully booked.

Since we kept getting new clients, we decided to expand to a larger space and hire more stylists. We have replicated that process several times over the last 10 years. The money was coming in, Rachel was fulfilling her calling, and we were enjoying life!

In fact, 2 years after we started, we were able to save enough money from our new salon business to get Rachel her dream car. As a young girl growing up, she always wanted a VW Beetle. In 2013, they came out with the new Beetle model, and we were able to pay cash for the limited 60's edition convertible turbo model. That year, we also treated ourselves to a 5-star all-inclusive vacation in Cabo San Lucas.

Young, in love, and things were beginning to look up. I don't tell you this to show off. I just tell you that story to let you know it's possible. If we could do it in a small town with small prices, you can do it too no matter where you're at.

2
The 3 Strategies to Grow Your Hair Business

Looking back, the game-changer in our business happened when I learned 3 strategies that I guarantee your beauty school didn't teach you.

It really is the easy button for growing your clientele, and I call it 'Clients on Demand.' By the way, these three strategies are the basic theory that you need to understand (and believe) before I can show you *how* it is done. I will show the step-by-step process in the next section.

Strategy 1: Find dream clients that want your service RIGHT NOW.

Something essential to understand is that 80% (give or take) of the women in your town already have a hairstylist they like and are loyal to. Even if you're going to provide a better cut and color than their current stylist, it really doesn't matter because they aren't looking for a new hairstylist. So going after EVERY woman in your city isn't very efficient and is a waste of your time.

You need to be marketing to the 20% that don't already have a hairstylist they love. This will save you time and money because you aren't trying to change people's minds; you are just offering your service to those that don't already have a hairstylist they love. This makes the whole thing a lot easier. These consist of people that are new to town, recently got a bad hair service, or maybe their hairstylist has retired or moved. No matter the reason, these people are prime and easy because they are already looking for a new hairstylist. All you have to do is be the FIRST ONE to get in front of them.

Notice that I said, 'first one.' In our small town, there are about 50 other hairstylists. In your city, there are probably more, maybe even up to 500 hairstylists. That means you have between 50-500 other competitors fighting for those 20%. The trick here is to be the first stylist these 20% see. If you can do that, the chances are really high, they will book an appointment with you. All you have to do is find the 20% and get in front of them where they spend most of their time; their phones. It works like clockwork and is the first key to getting clients on demand.

When we figured out this secret, it made adding new clients to our books every single day really easy!

Secret 2: Build instant trust with the 20% looking for a new hairstylist.

This one is essential and where most hairstylists get it wrong. You see, when you successfully get in front of a client, as I mentioned in Secret #1, you only have a few seconds to make that first impression where they feel comfortable and confident that their experience with you will be amazing.

It's just like online dating. Suppose you are looking for a potential date on Match.com. In that case, you're able to evaluate many things in a matter of seconds from their profile picture. Are they attractive? Do they look friendly? Do they look successful? Are they fun or stiff? Trustworthy or sketchy? It really only takes a few seconds to decide if you even want to take the next step just from their profile picture.

The same thing happens every time someone is looking for a new hairstylist. And there are 3 main things a new client is looking for in a new hairstylist: Someone that is trustworthy, competent, and likable. If your first impression on the Web exudes trust, competence, and likability, it is a no-brainer to schedule an appointment with you. And if you set up an automated system, new clients will be scheduling with you every day!

Most hairstylists don't know how to do this well on their own, and they're losing potential clients at this stage because clients look at their online presence and click the back button because the stylist didn't pass the trust, competence, and likeability test. So knowing HOW and WHERE to put your best foot forward is really important.

Quick review: Secret #1 is to be the first to get in front of the 20% of people in your area looking for new hairstylists. And when you successfully do that, Secret #2 is not to blow it with anything less than a top-notch first impression. This brings me to Secret #3.

Secret #3: Automate the whole process.

When we were just starting out, we tried the 'old school' methods of getting new clients, and that's where we struggled because the world is different now. Good old-fashioned hustle not only doesn't work as effectively, but it takes WAY too long to get any traction.

Imagine setting up a system once and letting that system bring you new clients on autopilot every single day without having to:

- Post new images on Instagram every day.
- Hustle your current clients to give you referrals.

- Lower your standards to get people's attention.

Here's the hard truth: You spent $15,000+ on beauty school, and you NEED to make this work.

But this career you signed up for has an 80% failure rate. So you may feel that you just crossed the finish line when you graduated from beauty school. But if you've been at this for any time, you know this is actually the starting line. And the choices you make right now will determine if you are in the 20% that succeed or the 80% that fail in this industry. That means, if you think back to your beauty school class, 8 of 10 will be broke within 1-2 years or working an hourly job at Great Clips or in an office somewhere. Was that the goal when you signed up to be a hairstylist?

The process of automation using your website ensures that you will not be one of the 20% that eventually call it quits.

3
The Buyer's Journey Marketing Funnel

Before you can begin designing a website, you need to understand the journey every person takes every time they buy a new product or service. I call it the buyer's journey. Understanding how this process works will help you craft your homepage in a way that moves visitors to become clients. I can say with absolute certainty that most salon websites have not even considered what you will learn in this chapter and therefore do not have websites that effectively turn visitors into clients. Implementing these tips will make your clientele-building process much quicker and smoother than your competitors.

There are 3 steps in the buyer's journey process:

- Awareness
- Desire
- Action

There are thousands of people in your city that don't know about you. They don't know who you are, and they don't know you are a hairstylist. There are probably hundreds each month that are looking for a new hairstylist. So the first step is showing them that you exist as a hairstylist. That is creating awareness. If no one ever becomes aware that you are a hairstylist, you will never even have the chance of getting a new client.

Once they know that you are a hairstylist, you need to create the desire to make you *their* hairstylist. Your website is the absolute best place to create that desire if done correctly. This includes a proper layout, design, the correct text, and images. I will show you *how* to do this in Part 3.

The goal with your website is to have a very high conversion rate, moving people from the desire to make you their hairdresser to actually scheduling an appointment. This is the 3rd step: Action. The more effective your website is at converting visitors to clients, the more appointments you will have, and the faster you will grow.

This is very important. Suppose your website has a 10% conversion rate. In that case, only 10% of the people that make it to your website will actually schedule an appointment. In other words, it will take you 10 times as long to build your clientele as it would if your website converted 100% of the visitors to clients. Obviously,

100% is virtually impossible, but a well-designed website can get you close.

Recently, I had my own buyer's journey for a robot vacuum. I was just scrolling through my Facebook newsfeed, and there was a video ad for a robot vacuum. We already have two upright vacuums in our house, so I was not in the market to buy another vacuum. But this video ad caught my eye; it was really demonstrative. I was captivated by the fact that it vacuumed in a systematic pattern, not random like other robot vacuums I had seen.

Now, I already knew robot vacuums existed. Still, this video ad made me aware of this particular brand and the unique benefits. I started thinking, 'Wow, I could actually set the timer and get my vacuuming done while I sleep and have a clean house when I wake up.' That desire was starting to grow inside me; they had me hooked. By the end of the video, I had to take action when they gave the 'limited time offer' of $100 off. So I clicked the buy button, and they made a sale.

That's how people buy things. No matter what you're buying, there's an awareness, a desire, and an action that takes place. You can go through the 3 steps of the buyer's journey in a matter of seconds like I did with the vacuum. Sometimes, the buyer's journey could take months with more significant purchases, like a house.

In the case of a salon or spa, the buyer's journey process is precisely the same. Many people in your city don't know that you exist, so the first step we're going to take is to create awareness by driving those looking for a hairstylist to your website. Once they have landed on your website, we're going to have the messaging right through text, images, and video, so that it creates a desire to make YOU their hairdresser. Then we will make it very easy for them to take action by creating an appointment. This process usually takes less than 2 minutes. Below is an illustration of how the sales funnel works.

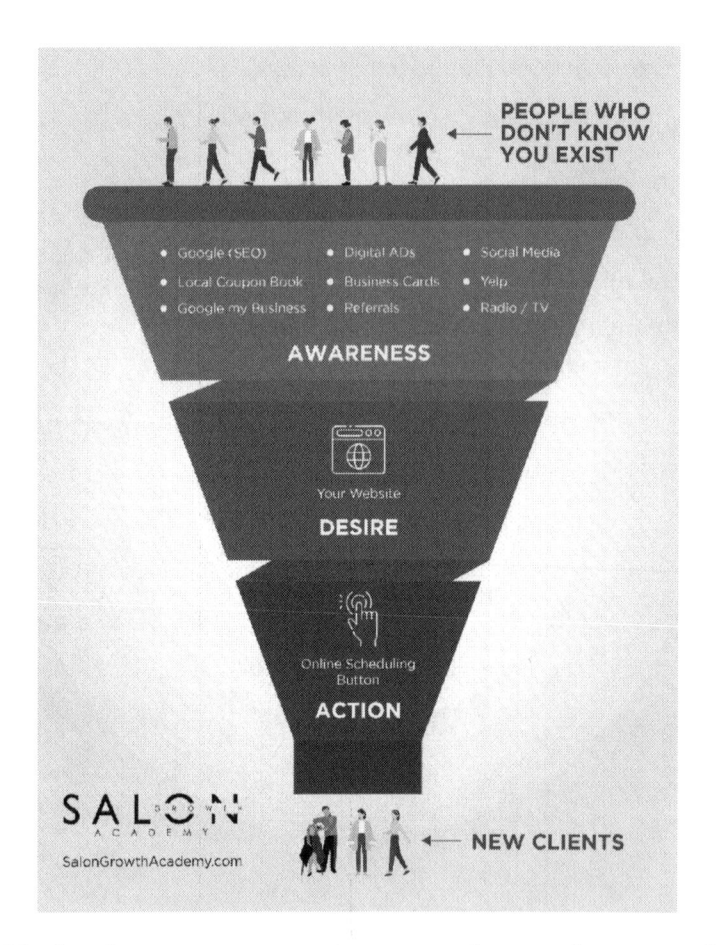

[Funnel diagram: People who don't know you exist → Awareness (Google SEO, Local Coupon Book, Google my Business, Digital Ads, Business Cards, Referrals, Social Media, Yelp, Radio/TV) → Desire (Your Website) → Action (Online Scheduling Button) → New Clients. SalonGrowthAcademy.com]

Notice there are many avenues to make people aware of you. I recommend using as many as possible so you can get as many people inside your funnel in the awareness phase. All platforms used to create awareness should drive people to your website where desire and action happen.

Part 2: What you need to know before you begin building the website

4
The Website Philosophy

I understand; you may already have a website. That's great. The chances are very high that your website is not designed to quickly turn visitors into clients. I don't say that to put you down. It is just that I have traveled to 37 states and visited hundreds of salon websites. In my experience, about 90% of the salon websites I have seen are almost worthless. Hopefully, by the end of this chapter, you will be able to identify some changes you need to make so that a high percentage of the people who visit your website become clients. Remember, the sole purpose of your website is to turn visitors into clients. Anything on your website that doesn't accomplish that needs to be eliminated.

While designing your website, the first thing to keep in mind is that people don't read websites; they scan them. You've seen people at the airport or at Starbucks scrolling with their thumb. There's so much information going into their mind that if it doesn't capture their attention immediately, they're moving on to the next thing. Our brains have been trained to constantly filter out information that will not benefit us.

In addition, if a web page takes too much time and energy to find what we are looking for, we click the back button. When this happens on your website, you have lost a potential client.

This is why we make our homepage simple, with professional images and short blurbs of text. People need to be able to land on your website, scroll it with their thumb, and make a decision to schedule an appointment in a matter of seconds.

Here's how you make your website simple, scannable, and a client-attracting machine that works for you 24/7.

Because people scan websites, you only have a few seconds to answer 3 simple questions, otherwise they will hit the back button, and you have lost a potential client. Those 3 questions are:

- Is this a hair salon?
- Will they give me an excellent hair service?
- How do I schedule an appointment?

Since you only have a few seconds to answer these questions, the answers need to be in the top section of your homepage before the scroll. This top section of the website is called *the hero section*. Let's go over each of these 3 questions that need to be answered in the hero section.

Question 1: Is this a hair salon?

The website visitor needs to know right away that they made it to a salon website. If the image or the text in the hero section doesn't make it clear that they landed on a salon website, they will click off your website. When I say this, it sounds like a no-brainer. You wouldn't believe how many salon websites make their hero image of the exterior of the building, or a field of flowers, or a peaceful stream, or something totally irrelevant. The imagery and text need to be congruent with the services you provide, so the visitor instantly knows you are a salon or spa.

Question 2: Will they give me an excellent hair service?

When people visit your website, they don't care about you (yet); they care about themselves. Are you going to make ME look good? Are you going to make ME feel special? If you spend the valuable space at the top of your website talking about your salon, your education, and why you are the best in town, you have missed the opportunity to connect with your audience. This is a huge mistake that most salon websites make. In one short sentence in the hero section of your website, tell them how you will make them look and feel if they schedule with you...and continue that customer service language throughout your homepage.

Question 3: How do I schedule an appointment?

Another common mistake I see is salon websites that don't have their phone number and/or an online scheduling button in the hero section. If you have executed the first two, but your potential client is clicking all over your website to find out how to schedule an appointment, you have lost them.

A way that you can test this out with your current website is to go to a coffee shop and, without being creepy, go up to a random stranger and ask if they have 1 minute to give you feedback on your website. Open your laptop/tablet to your homepage, give them 5 seconds, and close the laptop. Then ask her those three questions. If she can answer the three questions in the way that you were hoping, then you've done a good job!

In my Salon Website Academy course, I show a few examples of bad salon websites and give you a step-by-step over-the-shoulder view of my salon website build so that you can copy it for yourself or make it your own. To sign up for Salon Website Academy, visit SalonGrowthAcademy.com.

5
Choosing Website Images

Website images are critical because you're trying to put your best foot forward and build trust with potential clients so they will book a hair service. If your website images are anything less than professional, you aren't putting your best foot forward. Your website reflects you and your work, and a website with mediocre visual appeal tells the client your hair service is probably mediocre too. If you have beautiful website images, the potential client is more likely to trust you with their hair because they know you have good visual taste, take pride in your work, and pay attention to detail.

In addition to having professional images, you need to have congruent images. Your photos need to enhance the text you have next to them. If your text says, "We're here to make you look beautiful," and the image next to it is your salon with empty chairs, this is not congruent. A lot of salon websites make the 'empty chair' mistake. Instead, if your message is about beautiful hair, your image should have a happy woman that fits your target market with beautiful hair. By the way, there is nothing wrong with images showing off your salon. Show it off if you are proud of your salon design and decor. But make sure the text around that image is congruent, talking about your salon environment.

Next, most of your images (especially your hero image) need to have happy people in them. A common mistake is choosing a hero image of flowers, or a waterfall, or massaging rocks to give a peaceful feel. People don't connect with rocks; they connect with people. So to get them to connect and engage with your website, you need to have happy people in the images.

When people visit your website, they try to insert themselves into that situation. While an image of a waterfall is beautiful, it doesn't connect with your client looking for a hair service. But if your hero image is a picture of a woman smiling with beautiful hair, the website visitor will think, 'hey, I want to be like her. I want to be happy with beautiful hair.'

When choosing website images of happy people in them, I like to take your target demographic, then shave 5-10 years off. For example, if your target client is a retired 50+-year-old woman, you should use photos of women in their mid 40's experiencing salon or spa treatments. That way, website visitors think, 'that woman looks really pretty; I want to look like that.'

Conversely, if your website images are of 23-year-old supermodels, your 50-year-old target client will think you only service young women and will find a different hairstylist. It's ok to cheat a little bit on the younger side, but make sure that your images fit your target client demographic.

This brings up an important point. Before you even get started on your website, you need to consider your target demographic. Sure, your clientele will be made up of 17-year-olds and 71-year-olds. But take a good look at your community. Who do you connect best with? What stage of life are they in? Hone in on a target client, and pretend all your website text, images, fonts, and color palette connects with her.

Next, your website photos need to be professionally done. I mentioned this earlier, but you can't have your friend bring their iPhone in and take pictures of you doing a hair service. That's not going to cut it. Anything less than professional images will make your salon look really unprofessional and reflect negatively on your business. There are two ways you can accomplish this.

1. Hire a reputable professional photographer to take your website photos. There are a couple things you need to consider when choosing this option. You and your client models need to be comfortable and photogenic in

front of the camera. In addition, the photos should be taken at the end of the service when their hair is styled. In most cases, images of your client with wet hair in the cutting phase are not flattering. You will want to think through the messaging of your website so you can stage pictures that are congruent with your website message. Keep in mind a professional photoshoot in your salon can be several hundred dollars. But if it is done right, you can have some really great photos for your website and social media for years to come.

2. Purchase high-quality royalty-free photos, which you can purchase on websites like iStockphoto.com or Shutterstock.com. These royalty-free images are ones that you can buy the rights to and use freely on your website without violating any copyright laws. DO NOT take something off of Google images for free because you don't have permission to use those photos and could get slapped with a hefty fine by the owner of that image. I have heard stories of people being fined up to $10,000 for using a copyrighted photo on their website. Websites like iStockphoto.com and Shutterstock.com have professional images that you can purchase the rights to use on your website for $15-$30 per photo.

When downloading royalty-free photos from the internet, consider image size and resolution. Since you're putting these images on your website, page load speed is really important. If you have a huge image file, it will take more bandwidth when loading your web page and slow down your website. This hinders the user experience, especially on mobile devices. I recommend full-page images like your hero image should be no larger than 1400px (pixels) wide, and ½ page images (or less) should be smaller than 700px wide. For the quickest page rendering, all file sizes should be less than 1MB.

6
Getting Started With Squarespace

By this point, I bet you are feeling a bit overwhelmed. Take a deep breath; the rest of this book will be about implementation, and it is actually pretty easy if you follow me step-by-step.

When we first started our salon in 2011, you needed to hire a web developer or learn to use a complicated platform like WordPress or Joomla. In addition, you had to understand how to connect that site to a web server. The process had a big learning curve, was moderately expensive, and took a ton of time. On top of it all, your site would go down if one character was wrong in the code or database. It was a complete headache that prevented small salons or independent stylists from even trying.

With the web platforms available today, my dog could build a website. It is so much easier. Everything is done in one place and is very affordable with a small monthly payment. There are several simple platforms to choose from, but for the purposes of this training, I am going to show you how to build a website using a platform called Squarespace. I believe it is the easiest to use and will have all the features you need to create a beautiful website that converts visitors into clients.

Since I am building a mockup of a salon website, I will share the text and images I use in each section and why I used them. This is just an example, and I encourage you to take the concepts you learn in this book and apply them to craft the perfect messaging and design for your business. However, if you really like something I have written, I give you full permission to use it on your website.

These concepts will be new for most, and you may have a difficult time coming up with the right messaging for your website. That is ok. Be patient with yourself, and give yourself time. Sometimes it can take hours or even days to get the correct 4 words to use as the heading of your website. But once you get it right, it will pay dividends for years to come!

I have been doing this for a while, and it still takes me time brainstorming to get my message right to connect with my target audience. So be patient, don't get frustrated, and feel free to use or modify any examples I give while we build this website together. You can preview the finished website that we will be making by visiting SalonGrowthAcademy.com/website.

And like I have mentioned before, if you have not enrolled in my Salon Website Academy online video course, now is the time! In this training course, you will watch me set up a Squarespace account, design every section of the website, buy a domain name (i.e., www.yoursalonname.com) and even set up a branded email (i.e., yourname@yoursalonname.com). If you watch my training, pause the video and copy what you see me do, you can literally have your own beautiful website up and on the internet in the next 24 hours. Visit **SalonGrowthAcademy.com** to enroll.

Setting Up Squarespace

The first step is to create a Squarespace account. Go to Squarespace.com and click the 'Get Started' button in the top right for a free 14-day trial. Squarespace will ask you some questions about your business and give you an option to pick a website template. The template I used for this website build is called 'Bailard.' I chose that template because it has a large hero section and gives me good flexibility to add the 7 homepage sections I will be teaching about in the coming chapters.

You can click the 'preview' button on the templates page to see what a live example of that website would look like. Since I am using the Bailard theme, I will hover over it and click the link that says 'Start with Bailard.'

It will ask you to create an account. Go ahead and enter your email and a password. Once you have made a user, keep clicking 'Continue' at the bottom until your site is set up. It's that easy! Squarespace gives you 14 days to learn the platform and build your website for free. You don't even have to enter a credit card at this point.

Changing Website Colors

When starting a new website from scratch, the first thing I like to do is set the design elements like the color palette and default fonts. That way, I know any new pages or sections I create moving forward will have the same consistent look across the website.

On the left, click 'Design > Site Styles,' This will allow you to edit the fonts, colors, and other design elements site-wide.

I like to visit Pinterest or other sites that offer color palette ideas when choosing colors. You can find lots of ideas with a simple Google search. It is best if the color palettes offer a hex #. A hex number is a 6 digit code assigned to that specific color. In Squarespace, when you click 'Design > Site Styles > Colors > Edit Palette,' you will assign this unique 6 digit code to your color palette. You can play with different colors and see how they actually change the look of your website in real-time. If you have a hard time choosing colors for your website, Squarespace does have 18 color palette presets that you can choose from as well.

7
The Basics of Editing in Squarespace

One of the main reasons I recommend you use Squarespace is because it is incredibly easy to edit your website. In this section, I want to explain some of the basic edits that you will use all the time. If you make a change that you don't like, you can always click the 'undo' arrow (much like Microsoft Word), and it will restore your page to how it was before you made that change.

Creating Pages

The Squarespace template you chose will have a pre-made layout with several website pages already created by default. Of course, you will want to edit these or delete them entirely to match the website pages that you want. To add a new page, click the left sidebar that says 'Pages.' This will show you all of the current pages on your website. There are two sections now on the left sidebar in the 'Pages' section: 'Main Navigation' and 'Not Linked.' Any pages under 'Main Navigation' will appear in the top navigation bar of your website. In this section, you will want the most important website pages that you want your website users to see. Any pages that you want to have on your website but don't want to appear in the header navigation bar of your website should go under 'Not Linked.' You can easily rearrange any page on your website between these categories by simply clicking the page name and dragging it.

To create a new page for your website, click the '+' button, then 'Blank Page.' When you click the '+' button, it will give you several different options to choose from if you want to create a specific premade page layout. These are fun to experiment with. If you create a new page from one of these premade layouts and decide you don't like it, you can always delete it later.

Editing Pages

To edit a page on your website, simply click the page's name in the left sidebar, then click 'Edit' in the top left of that page. You are now in edit mode. Anytime you want to edit a section of text, just click the text you want to edit and begin editing. If you want to add a new section on your page, just hover your cursor between the two sections you want to add and click 'Add Section.' To change the section format, background, or colors, click the pencil icon in the top right of that section. To add a new element within the section, hover over the area you would like to add it and click the '+' icon. I.e., if you wanted to add a new image below some text, go to the text in that section, hover your cursor below the text, and a '+' icon will appear. Click that icon, and a box will pop up to allow you to add a variety of different forms of media. When you are happy with the changes you have made to your page, go to the top left, and click 'Done > Save.' The changes you make to your web page will not affect the live site until you save them in this way.

These are the basics of editing your website in Squarespace. Of course, you can make many additional customizations in Squarespace that I don't have time to go over in this chapter (it would be its own book). Spend some time trying things out and getting acquainted with the platform. Anything you create on accident can easily be deleted.

In the next part of this book, I will explain the 7 sections you must have on your homepage and the exact text I used (and why I used it) in those sections to build my salon website.

Following directions from a book can be more complicated than seeing it yourself. Sign up at SalonGrowthAcademy.com to watch me demonstrate how to assemble the 7 sections of this website in real-time. Let's get to building!

Part 3: The 7 Sections You Need on Your Homepage

In this part of the book, I will walk you through the 7 sections you should have on your homepage to build trust with potential clients, so they are moved to schedule an appointment with you. Hopefully, you are reading this book to create or modify your salon website. As a result, I want you to use this part of the book like an instruction manual. Read a chapter, then actually build that section of your website before moving on to the next chapter. This will ensure that you get the most out of it, and by the end of this book, you will have a finished website live on the internet that you can use to grow your business.

Visit SalonGrowthAcademy.com/website to follow along and see the finished homepage that I am creating with you in the following chapters.

8
The Hero Section

You know when you're going through the grocery store line, and you see those crazy magazines on the shelf like National Enquirer and Star? They always have some really wild claims right in the headlines with an image that catches your attention. I saw one recently that said, '40-year old man gives birth to twins.' We all know that 40-year old men can't give birth, but it piques our interest. Ok, maybe not your or my interest; we're smarter than that. But they sell magazines, so someone is buying them!

The whole point of the title and the image on the cover of that magazine is to get you interested so that you will buy. Well, that's the same thing we're going to accomplish with the header section of our website; capture attention, and move the user to action. Remember, in the first 5 seconds, you want your visitors to be able to answer three questions: Is this a hair salon? Will they give me an excellent hair service? How do I schedule an appointment?

In the hero section of my website, I chose a smiling woman with beautiful hair from iStockPhoto.com. Her face takes up the left half of the image, and she is looking to the right side of the Hero section, where my text overlay and online scheduling button will go.

A little marketing trick: since she is looking in the direction of the text and online scheduling button, it becomes the image's focal point. It forces the user to look there, which is exactly what I want them to do. That online scheduling button is the most important element of the Hero section of my website because this is how I get new clients and grow my salon. Everything on this website is designed to get the user to click the button and schedule a hair appointment.

The heading I chose to overlay this image is: 'LOVE YOUR HAIR - You Deserve to Look & Feel Your Best.'

There are a few reasons I chose the main heading, LOVE YOUR HAIR. It's only 3 words, so it's simple and easy to understand, and it passes the scroll test if someone is just scanning the website. Next, those three words tell you right away that this is a hair salon, which is the first question we need to answer.

The sub-heading, 'You Deserve to Look & Feel Your Best,' answers the second question, which is: will they give me an excellent hair service? I chose these words because we're actually addressing the problems that the potential client is experiencing. Yes, they need a haircut and color; that's why they are on our website to begin with. But deeper than that, this sentence helps them feel. A compelling message moves the audience to feel something and connect emotionally. So when I say, 'You Deserve to Look & Feel Your Best,' they begin to think, 'ya, I work hard. I owe it to myself. If I have to do my hair anyway, why not look my best?' We're connecting with them on an emotional level addressing their feelings. Not only will we make sure that you look good, but an experience at our salon will also make you feel your best. Maybe good hair salons in your area are a dime a dozen, but when you address their feelings, this can seal the deal!

The message is simple, straightforward and they know exactly what you want them to do next: click the button to book an appointment. For many, this is all they need to take that next step. But for those that aren't yet convinced, we still have 6 other sections on our homepage designed to move them to action.

Assignment:

Put the book down, and decide on the text and image you're going to use for the Hero section of your website. Let them know in just a few words that you are a salon that will give them an excellent hair service and how to schedule an appointment.

9
The FOMO & Value Proposition Sections

'The Pleasure Principle' is a concept by renowned psychologist Sigmund Freud. In a nutshell, Freud argues that all decisions humans make are to gain pleasure or avoid pain. The desire to avoid immediate pain is stronger and more motivating than gaining pleasure. We will use this understanding to create the messaging in this next section of our website.

On a salon website, it is pretty common to talk about the benefits of our salon: We are highly trained, use quality color, have a comfortable environment, have great prices, etc. But have you ever seen a salon website that addresses the pain someone will experience if they don't come to our salon? That is what the FOMO section is for.

FOMO stands for fear of missing out. FOMO is a real thing in our culture because people want to experience life to the fullest.

Imagine you are a big Justin Beiber fan, and Biebs announces his very last live performance ever is happening in your hometown. In addition, he said that he would be available for as long as necessary to meet and take pictures with anyone in attendance. As a Justin Beiber fan, this is a once-in-a-lifetime opportunity.

A strong message would be, 'don't be stuck at home alone while all your friends experience Justin Beiber's last live performance.' While there is no immediate pain to avoid here, there is a sense of urgency to not miss out on this once-in-a-lifetime experience.

In this section of our website, we want the user to consider what they have to lose or miss out on if they DON'T come to our salon. So the flow of the website will look like this: Come to our salon, and you will love your hair (Hero section). But if you don't come to our salon, your life will suck (FOMO section). But if you do come to our salon, here are a few more reasons you will love it (Value Proposition)!

Searching for a new hairstylist can be a scary thing. The prospective client is thinking: Will they cut my hair too short? Will my color not turn out? Will they add all kinds of extra charges? There are all kinds of questions and anxieties when choosing a new hairstylist. Use this to your advantage. Don't be afraid to address the things that could go wrong (at a different salon) in a tactful way.

Next, the value proposition section will highlight the unique benefits you have to offer.

If you have a unique message for each of these, feel free to give them their own section on your website. I decided to combine these into one section on my website because the messaging goes together nicely. I used the heading text of this section to address what would be lost and 3 icons with text below it for my value proposition.

The heading says, 'Life's Moments Are Too Important to Feel Blah. Treat yourself to beautiful, easy-to-manage hair!'

The message here is, if you don't get your hair done at our salon, you will feel average or mediocre. It gets them to think to themselves, 'I don't want to feel mediocre. I want to experience life to the fullest. When I meet new people, I want to feel confident. I want to feel at the top of my game, and I know that if I *look* good, I'm going to *feel* good.' Again, I am appealing to their feelings.

I want them to think about the important events coming up in the next few weeks of their life: A date, a wedding, dinner out with friends, an interview, a big presentation at work...the list is endless. Now, how do you want to feel at those critical moments in your life?

Mediocre? Unattractive? Inferior? Heck no! You want to feel beautiful, confident, happy, alive.

Many women sacrifice their potential beauty and confidence because they don't want to spend hours making their hair perfect every morning. So I wanted to address this by insinuating if this has been your experience, you are going to the wrong hairdresser. At our salon, we will help you find the best look for you and teach you a simple way to make it look good, so you can feel confident and happy without spending a ton of time on it every day.

Below is the value proposition. Think about 3 things that make your hair business unique, and use a little image/icon to illustrate this with some text underneath. Putting these blocks side by side in a row makes this section very easy to scan and can set your salon apart from other hair businesses.

For the value propositions, I chose:

- Clear Communication: We take the time upfront to understand your needs so that you leave with the look you have in mind.
- Superior Hair Service: Meet some of the most qualified hair stylists in Springfield who use the highest quality hair color.

- Friendly Environment: Lighten your load with people that care in a fun and relaxing atmosphere.

When brainstorming for this section, I created a list of people's fears when choosing a new hairstylist. I addressed the top three that I thought set our salon apart.

The reason for a bad cut or color is often in the lack of clear communication in the consultation process. Clients want to know that they are heard and that you understand what look they are going for. Many clients fear that they are going to explain what they want, and then you will end up doing something different. We want to put this fear to rest. So one of my messages in the value proposition is that we really take the time upfront to listen to what you want. We want them to trust that we are in business to serve them.

Next, I chose to address our skills to give them the peace of mind that we are also good at the technical part of the job. Let's not forget that this isn't all just emotional; they actually want a good haircut and color. So addressing that you are really good at what you do builds trust in your skill. You can talk about your five-star ratings in this section if you want. The message is, 'our clients always leave happy because we start with good communication, then execute what we talked about with an excellent hair service.' At the end of the day, we are performing a service, and when it comes to hair, people want to know they are working with the best.

Finally, I decided to speak about the environment in our salon. Something in the back of their mind is 'am I going to like my experience there? If they are going to spend 2-3 hours getting their hair colored, they want to know that they will enjoy the conversation and the salon's vibe. Some salons have a competitive atmosphere, and some stylists are emotionally exhausting. I wanted the last part of our value proposition to let them know that you will enjoy yourself at our salon. There won't be pressure or drama; it will be relaxing and pleasant. That's the reason I chose 'Friendly Environment' as the third part of my value proposition.

At the bottom of this section is another button to schedule an appointment online. You don't need to put a button in every section, but only one button at the top is not enough. I like to put 3-4 online scheduling buttons in different areas on the site, so if that section is what convinced them to book an appointment, they don't have to look far to take that step.

Assignment:

Put the book down, think through the text you're going to use for the FOMO and Value Proposition sections. What makes your salon unique? What makes you great?

10
The Authority Section

So far, we've done the first three sections: The header, the FOMO, and the value proposition sections. A lot of the heavy lifting has already been done. If you get those sections right, by themselves, you're going to convert a lot of visitors into clients, which is a really great thing. The rest of the website is for potential clients who want to dig deeper and learn a little more about you. They're here, you've got their attention, but they're not really ready to schedule an appointment quite yet. They want to learn more, and that's what these following sections are about.

As a result, the order of these next sections is not as important as just getting them right. I've chosen to use a video and text layout in the authority section of the website. The video is only 30-seconds long, and it has about 15 short clips in the salon with a voiceover. This is actually the video that I teach you to make in Salon Video Academy. I love using video for marketing. It really brings another dimension to your business and effectively builds trust with the client. That is why I think a video is perfect in the authority section. The first

3 sections let them know that they are in good hands, but the video takes it home by showing your competence. Most salons don't go the extra mile to produce a promotional video, so if you can pull it off, it will really set you apart in your city.

I also put a heading with a short paragraph to the right of the video. It says: "What Makes Nine Salon Great? We understand that choosing a new hairstylist can be scary. Will they screw up my hair? Will I be trapped into a hairstyle that I don't like? Will they listen to me? At NINE Salon, we take the time to listen to what you want and have the skills to make you look and feel your best."

At this point in your website, people want to know what sets this salon apart from other salons? So we're simply affirming what we already mentioned in the top sections. But people need to hear the same thing repeatedly to believe it. The message doesn't always sink in the first time, so a lot of your website will just repeat what you've already said differently.

Notice in this section we also said, "Choosing a new hairstylist can be scary." We're addressing the fear that a lot of people have. When people find a hairstylist they love, they will stick with them for life. But change happens. People move, or their hairstylist retires. There are many reasons that your prospective client finds herself in the place of looking for a new hairstylist. One negotiation strategy is to address the fears the other party has in making the deal. If you get it out in the open, the thing they were afraid of loses its power. That's what we are doing here.

Back to the video. I like using a video in the authority section because websites are pretty static, and a video brings a different dimension of life to the website. The visitor will be able to learn a lot more about your salon. They would be able to see your face, hear your voice, and often times this makes a connection if there wasn't one before. There are many things that a video can do that text and images on the website can't, so that's why I love having a video on the website.

I like to make two types of videos for this section, and they are pretty easy to make with your smartphone if you know what to do. The first is an interview-style video where you answer a few questions about your business, passion, and expertise. You will talk about what sets you apart and include much of what you put in your value proposition. Finish by adding a clear call to action to schedule an appointment. Include some short 'action shots' of your work in the salon over the interview clips. The whole point of the video is to build likability and trust and usually lasts 60-90 seconds.

The next video is more of a short commercial voiceover video. All you have to do is take 10 to 15 different 5-second clips of you doing hair or having fun with your clients. Maybe add some shots of your salon equipment and decor so they can see the environment before they arrive. This eases any anxiety they may have at going to a new salon. You will put these clips together and lay the voiceover on top of the clips with some upbeat (royalty-free) music in the background. Always be sure to end the video explaining how to schedule an appointment. If you decide to offer a special discount or something, the end of the video is the time to do it. This video affirms the things already on the website and is usually about 30 seconds long. You can see the example I made at

SalonGrowthAcademy.com/website.

Assignment:

Put the book down, think through the text you're going to have in the authority section, and write out a 30-second script for a video voiceover. Tell your visitor why you are qualified to do their hair. You're building trust, addressing any fears, and letting them know you are an expert. Notice this is the first time that you're talking about yourself. Everything has been talking about the client up to this point, but now you can begin to let them know why you are their best choice.

I understand the idea of making a video can be a little bit intimidating, so I want to break this down for you. If you've never created a video like this before, let's start with the voiceover video. All you have to do is get out a piece of paper and brainstorm about 10 different shots in your salon of you in action and various locations in your salon. If you do waxing, maybe have somebody getting their eyebrows waxed. Think through different scenes that you can use and write them down. Then create a 30-second script which will be 4-5 short sentences. Use any video editing software to put those clips together, lay down the background music, and voiceover. That's it! If you need my help creating your promotional video, please reach out using the contact form at SalonGrowthAcademy.com/contact.

11
The Action Steps Section

There are 4 sections left on your website. This bottom half of your website is for people who still want more information and will spend more time reading about your salon.

It should come as no surprise, but people want to spend less time and energy thinking for themselves. In the Action Steps Section, you will tell the visitor what you want them to do in 3 easy steps. I am giving them 3 easy steps to schedule an appointment with us in this case.

You may think that you have already been clear enough about scheduling an appointment in previous sections, so this section isn't necessary...but you would be wrong. Remember, people are scanning your website, and they may have missed something. So even though it may seem redundant, you need to hold their hand and give them the step-by-step instructions to schedule an appointment.

Remember Geico's ad campaign, 'It's so easy, even a caveman can do it'? They spent millions of dollars sending us the message that signing up for an insurance policy online is easy. They did that because they knew they would get more people to click over to their website and fill out the free online quote if they sent the message that it is easy. That is precisely the same strategy here. Some people are afraid that they may do something wrong in the online scheduling process. So we take the already easy online scheduling process and break it down into 3 steps. It takes the mystery out of the process and makes them comfortable taking that next step.

In my example website, I say:

"Scheduling an Appointment is Easy!"

Step 1: Click the button below.

Step 2: Choose a stylist and service.

Step 3: Pick your date & time.

There is something about taking an unknown process and breaking it down into 3 simple steps that makes people feel more comfortable. Look at the steps I listed above; they are easy: Click, pick a service, pick your time. Someone reads those steps and gets a boost of confidence, thinking, 'I can do that,' and they schedule an appointment. Put yourself in a prospective client's shoes. They are already afraid of finding a new hairstylist, and they don't know you. This is their first time on your website. So if the action steps are clear and straightforward, they will be more likely to take action. That is all we are trying to do in this section.

In addition, this is just a fundamental principle of sales. You can have a wonderful presentation about your product, and people may fall in love with it. But if you don't actually ask them to buy, many won't buy. The principle is the same here: Many won't take action if you don't actually ask them directly to book an appointment.

Assignment:

Put the book down, and create 3 simple action steps that you want the visitor to make. Make it so clear and simple, even a caveman could do it.

12
The Testimonial Section

Social proof is the psychological process that gets someone to do something because they see someone else doing the same thing. In other words, if everyone else is doing it, I should too. You've heard it said, "Word of mouth is the best form of advertising." It's true. Social proof is a powerful persuasion tool used in marketing. There is no better way to do this on your website than through positive client testimonials.

When you shop for something online, you probably read the reviews before you purchase because you want to see if the product actually measures up to how it was advertised. The same is true for your prospective client.

Until this point, they have scanned your website and may think, 'ya, you said a lot of really nice things about yourself, but how do I know they're true?' The testimonial section is used to validate the positive things you have said about your salon from someone who has actually received a hair service from you. The prospective client reads the testimonial of someone else having a great experience, so it must be true. People have been conditioned to rely on testimonials when making a purchase decision.

There are a couple ways you can display testimonials: text or video. If you can get quality video testimonials, do it. But if you can't, text will do the trick. I always include the first name and last initial of the person giving the testimonial, so readers know it's a real person without compromising the person's identity. And if you can get permission to use the person's headshot above the testimonial, even better.

Regarding testimonials, I recommend including 1-5 on your website. One testimonial on your page is all you need to satisfy social proof, but if you can get a few more, it will validate your message even more. Anything more than 5 will probably clutter your website unless they are on a timed scroller. People can always visit your Google, Yelp or Facebook pages to read more testimonials.

If you already have great testimonials on your social media that you can copy and paste, that is great. But I would encourage you to go to a few of your favorite clients and ask if they would be willing to write you a positive review, and then coach them on what you are looking for. Of course, you can't tell them what to say, but you can coach them on how to say it using this format:

1. Address some sort of problem they were experiencing before they started coming to you for hair services.
2. Why they choose to trust you with their hair.
3. What positive results or experiences they have had since you have been doing their hair.

It is the before and after process: What was their life like before coming to you for hair, and what was their life like after. Showing positive transformation is the most powerful testimonial, and it only needs to be 2-4 sentences long.

Here are a couple examples of a good client testimonial:

"My hair is very fine, and it has always been a challenge to get my style right. I am so excited to find [Your Name] at [XYZ] salon. She was so patient with me during the consultation to find a style that would work for me. This is the best haircut I have ever had. I am so happy I found [Your Name]."

"Finding a new hairstylist is such a hard thing for me because I have had some bad hair color experiences in the past. I recently got a balayage and haircut with [Your Name] at XYZ salon, and couldn't be more pleased. The color turned out perfectly, and I love my new hairstyle. I am so glad I won't have to find a new hairstylist anytime soon."

If you don't coach your client on how to write the testimonial, the chances are good that it will not be what you want. Unfortunately, I had to learn this the hard way, especially when doing video testimonials because people feel on the spot in front of the camera. Then you end up with a nervous person trying to find their thoughts and not really saying anything meaningful, even though they love you. The last thing you want is to ask your client to write or do a video testimonial for you and then not use it because it doesn't meet your standards. And by the way, you should have standards; this is your website and your livelihood we are talking about. So make sure you coach them on the format. Your client will feel more confident in what you asked them to do, won't ramble with unnecessary information, and you will end up with gold for your website.

Assignment:

Put the book down, and contact 3-5 of your favorite clients to ask them for a positive testimonial that you can use on your website. Walk them through the format above, so their testimonial is effective at convincing prospective clients to book an appointment with you.

13
The Cover Letter Section

Your website has been very scannable with images and very little text until this point. Most of the content has been about the client and what they want. This is the section where you can talk about you and your salon like you would with a cover letter when applying for a job.

We put this section at the bottom of the website for a reason. If they still haven't made up their mind about you, they're crazy because you have a fantastic website…but this is the last chance to put your best foot forward.

Some things you could talk about in this section include:

- What you specialize in, or what kind of services you love doing.
- What they will experience in your salon.
- The salon atmosphere.
- Your salon mission or values.
- Anything that will make you look good that the client needs to know.

This section doesn't need to be long; 2-5 paragraphs is sufficient. The other thing that this part of your website does is it helps with your search engine optimization or SEO. When Google crawls your website, it looks for words that explain what your website is about. You want to write this section for your client, but keep Google in mind. Google is looking for what kind of business you are and the location. Find a way to work those keywords in there for Google's sake. More on making your site Google-friendly in the final part of this book.

Assignment:

Put the book down, and write the Cover Letter paragraphs of your website.

14

The Lead Generation Section

Finally, the last section of your website is the Lead Generation Section. The point of this section is to capture the name and email address of people who came to your website but didn't schedule an appointment. This allows you to continue the relationship until they decide to book an appointment in the future.

You could send them free tips and tricks for their hair or promote products and services. This helps potential clients get to know you better so they will feel comfortable scheduling an appointment with you later on.

Building this section is slightly technical, but here's how it works. First, you will sign up for a free email marketing platform like Mailchimp or Constant Contact. You will then connect this service to this section of your website. When someone enters their name and email in the form, it automatically gets added to your Mailchimp list. You can create pre-drafted emails that get sent out automatically when someone gets added to the list. Or you can send an email to your entire list to promote products or services that you offer.

Well, there you have it. We have explained the 7 sections that you need to have a well-designed website that works for you 24 hours a day to turn visitors into clients. Hopefully you have stopped between chapters and built out each website section. Again, I give you full permission to use my example website content. Or if you just want me to build and maintain the example website for you for a small monthly fee, visit SalonGrowthAcademy.com/website and click the green bar at the top of the page.

15
My Case For Online Scheduling

Online scheduling is a critical catalyst to the growth of your business! In 2011 when it wasn't even that popular yet, it was a must-have for our salon, and we haven't looked back. It has proven to be our secret weapon in growing our clientele quickly, so I am a HUGE advocate for online scheduling on your website. There are several reasons you need an online scheduling option if you don't already have one.

First of all, did you know that 70% of people prefer scheduling appointments online instead of over the phone? It is essential to give clients that option from a customer service perspective. If you are trying to grow your clientele and don't have an online scheduling option for clients, you are missing out on multiple new appointments per day. This one simple change in your business could help you grow much faster than you are right now.

Next, online scheduling will save you a lot of time managing your clients, their appointments, rescheduling, cancellations, etc. How much time do you spend on the phone doing these administrative tasks? That time could be spent working, with family, or however you want to spend it.

And you aren't the only one wasting time. Think of how your client feels when the only option they have to reschedule an appointment is through text message. You are busy doing hair, so they don't hear back from you for 2 hours. Then you give them a few rescheduling time slots, and those don't fit their schedule, so you need to find another one that works. It could take 15 text messages back and forth over the entire day just to simply reschedule an appointment. And that's just one client! It's completely inefficient.

Online scheduling allows you to empower your clients to handle their own appointments. Not only can they make appointments from their client dashboard, but they can also cancel or reschedule appointments. Most clients like the freedom and flexibility to do this on their own time and not be limited to your business hours and availability, so it is a win/win.

Another benefit of online scheduling is automated client reminders via text message and email. If you haven't figured it out yet, I want you to automate anything you can in your business so you can focus on your clients, your family, and yourself. No-shows are a part of the business because let's face it, people are flaky. Appointment reminders significantly lower the percentage of no-shows. You could spend 20 minutes each evening making appointment reminder phone calls…or you could save 20 minutes of your life each night and let the automated software do it for you! I want to encourage you to begin working your way to completely removing the phone from your business.

And while we are talking about automation, saving time, and getting new clients, think about this. Someone in your city had a busy day and forgot that she needs to get her hair done for an important interview she has next week. But it's 10:30pm. There isn't a salon in town that will answer her phone call. But in her search, she lands on your website and sees the online scheduling button. She clicks it, looks at all of your available appointments before her interview, and makes an appointment. You just got a new client while you were sleeping! The client is extremely thankful that you had that option, and you are happy because the software is helping you grow your business 24/7/365.

I remember how this concept clicked with me when we first started out. Every appointment mattered because, when you are growing, there are days that you don't even have one appointment scheduled. This was one of those days, and we went to bed with no hair appointments on the schedule. To our surprise, when we woke up the following day, there were 2 new cuts and colors on the schedule. That day alone, we earned a couple hundred dollars that we would not have made without online scheduling...and this happens day in and day out. The amount of money that you can earn when you have a machine working for you all the time is massive compared to doing it all yourself.

So which online scheduling software should you use? There are a lot of great ones out there that are specifically for salons. The one that I like the best and have used since 2011 is called Rosy Salon Software. The reason I like it is that it's really inexpensive to use. Just for the online scheduling features alone, it's well worth it. But Rosy does so much more. It is a cloud-based salon management suite that keeps track of your schedule, client records, employee management, point of sale, credit card processing, retail and professional inventory, automated SMS appointment reminders for clients and employees, salon sales reports, and lots more. Since it is cloud-based, you can have access on any device with an internet connection.

If you are interested in giving it a try, you can get a 30-day free trial to Rosy Salon Software when you use my special link: https://www.rosysalonsoftware.com/features?vid

=15004. When you use this link to sign up, you can also reach out to me if you need any help getting your online scheduling set up on your website.

Here is the thing: online scheduling is meant to be used on your website. So if you don't have a website, the ability to use the growth benefits of online scheduling to their maximum potential is impossible. Sure, you could post your online scheduling link on your Instagram or Yelp profile. But I believe the most effective flow of traffic is 3rd party profile (IG, FB, Yelp, etc.) to your website, to your online scheduling. This allows potential clients to warm up to you by visiting your website. They usually can't do this from a social profile. So, you need a website so you can use the benefits of online scheduling. But there is no point in having online scheduling unless you have a well-designed website. They work together magically!

In the next part of this book, I will show you some of the best methods we've used to get prospective clients to our website so they can schedule an appointment. This process also is automated. So if you can automate the process of getting your target client to your website, automate their experience on your website, and automate the appointment scheduling , you can literally take yourself out of the entire process of getting new clients. It is just a matter of setting up simple automated systems to do the work for you day in and day out. I'll show you how in the next section!

Part 4: The Top of the Marketing Funnel

16
Getting Website Visitors

You have finished your website. Well done! You may feel that you've passed the finish line, but actually, you are just getting started. Just because you have a website live on the internet doesn't mean anyone will visit the website. The only way your beautiful website can do the job it was created to do is if potential clients in your city make it to your homepage. Then, and only then, can we convert them to clients and grow your business.

I could actually write an entire book on this topic (and maybe I will), but I want to give you a crash course on finding qualified potential clients and driving them to your website in this final chapter.

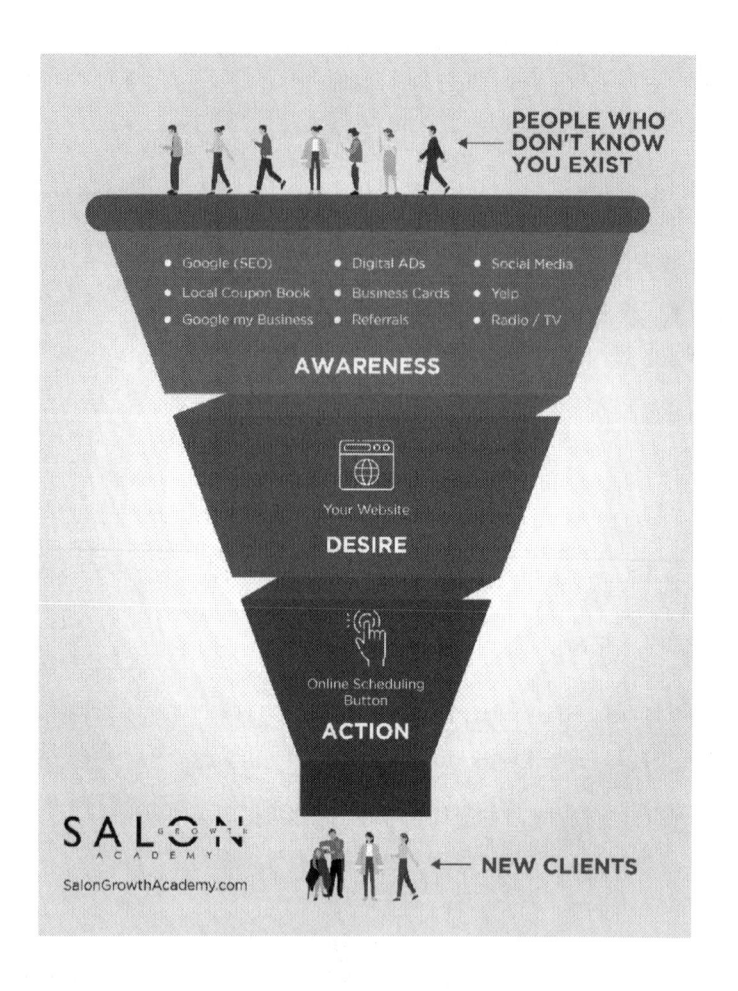

As you can see, there are lots of different ways to drive prospective clients to your website (The awareness phase). People could get to your website from a business card, your social media profiles, directory profiles like Yelp and Google My Business, referrals, digital advertisements like Facebook, Instagram,

Google, your local chamber of commerce website, and many other ways. You need to decide which methods will give you the most traffic to your website for the least amount of money. I want to share the methods I have used and what I think are the best for growing your business.

Search Engine Optimization (SEO)

Maybe you have heard this term before. SEO is the process of optimizing your website, so it is 'Google-friendly.' Google is constantly crawling all websites on the internet and indexing them in its algorithm. The goal is to employ SEO best practices so that Google ranks your website at the top of the search results when someone is searching for a new hairstylist in your city.

This is the #1 way we get 30-40 new clients each month in our salon. When people in our city do a Google search for a hair salon, our salon website comes up as #1 in the search results. People click on our website and schedule an appointment. It is as easy as that, and this method has worked day in and day out for the last 10 years without costing us a penny.

Pros:

- It is totally organic, so if you know what you are doing, it doesn't cost a penny; only your time.

Cons:

- This works best in smaller to medium-sized cities. If you work in a large city, it will be much more difficult to rank in the top positions of Google search because there are so many other salons in your area competing for the same thing.
- It takes time to see results. It often takes 3-6 months to see your website rank in the first few positions of Google.

Digital Ads

If you aren't getting many potential clients to your website organically, you can simply pay to get potential clients to your website. This is done by paying for digital advertisements on Google, Facebook, Instagram, and other platforms. These advertising platforms have incredible targeting capabilities, so you can really hone in your audience, so the ads are only being served to the people you want.

Let's say your target audience is a 36-year-old female in your city with a household income of more than $100,000. You can actually send your ads to this exact demographic if you want. I know; it's scary what kind of information Google and Facebook have on us! Since you can pinpoint your audience, you can keep your ad costs low.

I always recommend starting with a low budget of $10 per day to test. If your ads prove to work and you begin getting clients from your advertising, increase your daily ad spend by $10 increments until you get the results you want.

If you want to learn how to use these advertising platforms yourself, I have an online course called Salon Traffic Academy available on my homepage at SalonGrowthAcademy.com. If you just want to hire me to manage your digital advertising, fill out the form at SalonGrowthAcademy.com/contact.

Pros:

- You can pinpoint your audience.
- You can get results immediately.

Cons:

- There is a learning curve for effectively running ads and using the platforms.
- It costs money.

Google My Business

Google My Business is a directory profile that any business can (and should) sign up for. If you search for a salon in your City, State, there will be a section at the top of the search results that lists 3 local salons with pins showing locations on the map. These 3 listings are populated by the Google My Business listing.

Google My Business listings are free to create. You should fill out the profile as complete as possible with your business information, description, operating hours, pictures, etc. When you first create a listing, it is not totally finished until it is verified. Google will send you a postcard in the mail with a code. You then log in to your Google My Business profile and enter the code to verify your listing. They do this to make sure that your business is legit and in the location that you say it is.

Since Google only shows 3 local salons in this section of the search results, becoming one of those 3 salons is REALLY important for getting free organic traffic to your website. If you can rank your Google My Business listing in one of these 3 positions, you will get new potential clients visiting your website every day.

Google My Business has added a new feature where certain online scheduling platforms, like Rosy, offer an online scheduling button right there on the listing. So people can actually schedule an appointment right from the Google search results without even going to your website. Anytime you can streamline the scheduling process, by all means, do it!

Ranking your Google My Business listing falls in the SEO category, and if you want help with this, you know how to reach me!

Pros:

- It is free to create.
- If you rank in the top 3 salons, it could bring many new clients to your website.

Cons:

- None. If you haven't created your profile, get after it!

Online Directory Profiles

An online directory profile is anywhere on the internet where you can put your business name, address, phone, and website URL. There are hundreds of online directory profiles that you can sign up for, like Yelp, YP, Manta, etc.

On a majority of these sites, it's free to create a profile, and I recommend you do so. Often, when someone does a Google search for a hair salon in your area, Yelp and other third-party directories will come up in the search results. If you have a free listing on these platforms, potential clients can find your business and click over to your website, where they can schedule an appointment.

Most of your competition has a profile on the big ones like Yelp and YP, but most won't go further than that. I recommend signing up for profiles on 30-40 directories. This ensures your business is spread out over the internet. The more places potential clients can find you, the better.

For some of these directories, there is a paid option. Generally speaking, I don't think they are worth it and are not where I would put my advertising dollars.

Take Yelp, for example. If you have a free profile on Yelp, you will probably get sales calls a couple times per year trying to get you to buy their paid advertising. I don't recommend paying for Yelp ads because I don't like their pricing structure and don't trust the metrics they provide on their sales calls. They once told me that more people were viewing my Yelp profile than the population in my city. So I just don't trust their data and think your ad budget is better spent on the platforms listed above.

Pros:

- Signing up for directory profiles is free.
- These profiles can help your Google ranking.

- Some people use these platforms to find hairstylists.

Cons:

- The occasional sales call.

Everything Else

If you look at the top of my funnel diagram, there are many other ways to get potential clients to your website so they can become a client. I'm sure you can think of more ways that I didn't list in my funnel. The purpose of this chapter is to touch on what I believe are the most effective methods so you can begin getting the most traffic to your website with the least amount of time and money.

Just like your business will earn more money with multiple revenue streams (service, retail products, upsells, etc.), you will get more clients with multiple 'top-of-the-funnel' methods to create awareness and drive traffic to your website. Get in front of as many potential clients from as many avenues as possible, and use those avenues to drive them to your website.

17
Hire Dustin For Your Salon Marketing

Final Thoughts

Thanks so much for reading this book. Helping salon and spa professionals get more clients and grow their business is my passion, so I am genuinely grateful that you took the time to read this book. I trust that the information you have learned will help you with your digital marketing so you can automate new clients in your chair.

While the purpose of this book is to give you the tools to do it all yourself, I realize you may prefer to have it done for you, so you don't have to think about it. As a result, I am providing a list of services and online courses I offer with links to sign up for those services.

Templated Web Design - $97/mo

I realize many independent hairstylists don't have a large budget for their website, but I don't think this means you should have to sacrifice quality. That's why I've designed a beautiful website template, especially for hairstylists and spa professionals. I have meticulously thought through every word and image on the page to bring you a website that you'll be proud of and will turn visitors into clients. I will make this exact website for you and change the logo and contact information to fit your business. Since we are not starting from scratch, you get the best of both worlds: a beautiful website in a few days that is very affordable even for an independent hairstylist.

Visit SalonGrowthAcademy.com/website to see the exact website you will get in this package, and click the green bar at the top to place your website order.

Customized Web Design - Starting at $2000 + $97/mo

This option is for the salon or spa that wants to start from scratch and design a beautiful website that fits their brand. We will work together on the messaging and imagery to get you the look you will love.

Fill out the form at SalonGrowthAcademy.com/contact and schedule a call with me to get started.

Website Search Engine Optimization - (SEO)

I will optimize your website and work monthly to increase your website ranking in Google search, so prospective clients find you first when looking for a new hairstylist. Many factors determine the difficulty of ranking your website, and plans typically start at $300/mo.

Fill out the form at SalonGrowthAcademy.com/contact and schedule a call with me to get started.

Google/Facebook/Instagram Ads

If you want to be aggressive in driving qualified leads to your website, paid digital advertising is the best way. I will do a complete analysis and recommend the best advertising solution for your business. Your advertising budget must be a minimum of $3000/mo for this option to make sense.

Fill out the form at SalonGrowthAcademy.com/contact and schedule a call with me to get started.

Video Production

Making a professional promotional video is one of the best ways to build trust with potential clients. I produce professional 30-90 second videos to do just that, and I charge $1000 per finished minute of video.

Fill out the form at SalonGrowthAcademy.com/contact and schedule a call with me to get started.

Online Courses

I realize that hiring out marketing services can be outside the budget for some, so I have created an online course for each of the above services. If you want to do it yourself, you can learn the skills through the step-by-step process I use.

Salon Website Academy - Learn to build your own website.

Salon Traffic Academy - Learn SEO, Google Ads, and Facebook ads.

Salon Video Academy - Learn to make a promotional video using your smartphone.

You can sign up for any of these courses at SalonGrowthAcademy.com or bundle all 3 for a discount.

No matter what you choose to do, I wish you all the best in your career and many blessings in your life.

Make today extraordinary!

Dustin

Made in the USA
Las Vegas, NV
23 June 2022